CAMBRIDGE TO ELY

including St.Ives to Ely

RICHARD ADDERSON
and
GRAHAM KENWORTHY

MP Middleton Press

Cover picture: Class D16/3 4-4-0 no. 62566 stands in one of the bay platforms at Cambridge, ready to head north towards Ely with a stopping passenger train on 30ᵗʰ June 1951. The first coach of its train gleams in the new British Railways livery, contrasting with the vehicle on the right, which still retains its LNER paint and numbering. The engine shed, with its smoke chutes and distinctive northlight roof, provides the backcloth to this atmospheric scene. (G.Powell / GERS collection)

Readers of this book may be interested in the following society:
Great Eastern Railway Society, J.R.Tant, Membership Secretary, 9 Clare Road,
Leytonstone, London E11 1JU

Published October 2005

ISBN 1 904474 55 1

© *Middleton Press, 2005*

Design Emily Pede

Published by
    Middleton Press
    Easebourne Lane
    Midhurst, West Sussex
    GU29 9AZ
Tel: 01730 813169
Fax: 01730 812601
Email: info@middletonpress.co.uk
www.middletonpress.co.uk

Printed & bound by Biddles Ltd, Kings Lynn

CONTENTS

1. St Ives to Ely (Sutton Branch Junction) 1- 44
2. Cambridge to Ely   45-120

INDEX

85	Barnwell Junction	4	Needingworth Junction
7	Bluntisham	1	St. Ives
45	Cambridge	39	Stretham
87	Chesterton Junction	18	Sutton
78	Coldham Lane Junction	43	Sutton Branch Junction
12	Earith Bridge	96	Waterbeach
104	Ely	102	West River
103	Ely Dock Junction	34	Wilburton
28	Haddenham		

ACKNOWLEDGEMENTS

In addition to the photographers acknowledged in the photographic credits, we are most grateful to A.Rush and M.Storey-Smith for their assistance in the compilation of this book. The Great Eastern Railway Society has produced a series of CDs of material that is to be found in the National Archive at Kew; these have proved extremely useful in researching detailed background information.

Railways of the area in 1922 at a scale of approx 1 inch to 7½ miles. Other maps in this volume are to a scale of 25 ins to 1 mile, unless otherwise stated.

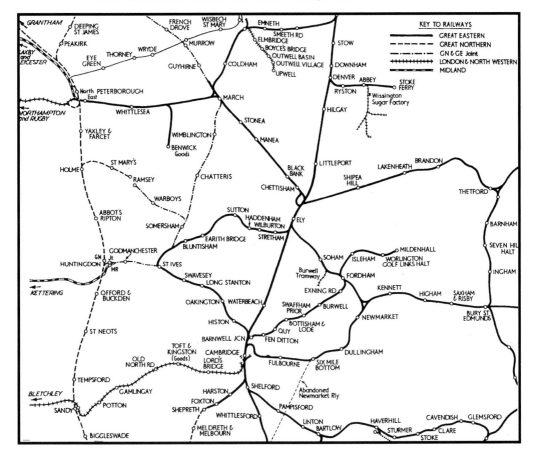

GEOGRAPHICAL SETTING

Cambridge to Ely

As it reaches the north-eastern suburbs of the City of Cambridge, almost exactly two miles north of the station, the railway crosses the River Cam. For the next ten miles the river remains to the east of the line, sometimes a few yards away, never more than a mile distant. Along this section the route is almost straight and passes through rich agricultural fen country, which, at times, stretches as far as the eye can see in all directions. Just over three miles from Ely station the River Great Ouse (known locally as the West River) is bridged; a short distance to the east of the bridge, the Cam and Great Ouse converge for their onward journey to the Wash at Kings Lynn.

St Ives to Ely

In contrast to the main line, this branch meandered across the countryside on fairly level gradients, not only to provide access to the fertile fenland, but also to serve several village communities which had developed over the centuries on the "islands" of Kimmeridge Clay which rise from the peat fens. This led to a somewhat circuitous route, the only noticeable gradients occurring where the line skirted the clay outcrops or rose and fell to cross watercourses. However, because the line followed what is, in effect, a valley floor, the elevated communities that it served were located some distance away. This was relatively unimportant in the pre-motorised Victorian era, but became increasingly relevant as the age of the internal combustion engine progressed.

The gradient diagrams date from the GER period. However, as a result of later surveys, the gradients may be slightly different from those shown on gradient posts in more recent times.

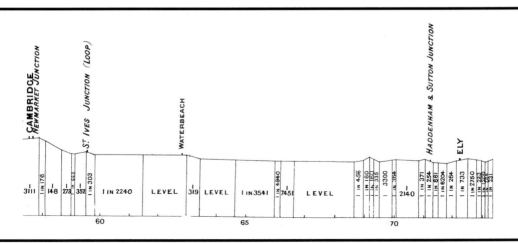

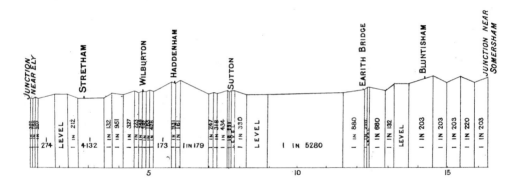

HISTORICAL BACKGROUND

Cambridge to Ely

The Great Eastern Railway referred to the whole length of the main line from London to Norwich via Cambridge as the "Cambridge Main Line". A more detailed account of the origins of the whole line appears in our earlier volume *Ely to Norwich*. The 15 mile section from Cambridge to Ely formed part of the Eastern Counties Railway's contribution to the route, linking the Northern & Eastern Company's line from London, which had reached only as far as Bishops Stortford, with the Norfolk Railway at Brandon. The section of double track from Bishops Stortford through to Norwich opened on 30th July 1845. By 1884 junctions with five branch lines had been made between Cambridge and Ely as can be seen on the map; three of them were immediately north of Cambridge, while the other two joined to the south of Ely station.

The Great Eastern Railway passed into the ownership of the London & North Eastern Railway on 1st January 1923, and the line became part of the Eastern Region of British Railways upon Nationalisation on 1st January 1948.

Immediately following Privatisation in 1997, services between Cambridge and Ely were provided by Central Trains and West Anglia & Great Northern, in both cases as part of much longer routes. A further operator appeared on the scene in 2002 when Anglia Railways introduced a through service from Cambridge to Norwich; the franchise for this service passed to **one** Railway during 2004. The trains of a variety of freight operators have been seen on the line including those of EWS, GB Railfreight and Freightliner.

St Ives to Ely

The first section of the line to be built, from Ely to Sutton, a distance of approximately seven miles, owed its existence largely to two local major landowners. They were anxious to find a more efficient outlet for their produce than that available via the somewhat primitive tracks and roads of the area. The Bill for the Ely, Haddenham and Sutton Railway had a smooth Parliamentary passage in the 1863/4 Session, the Act being passed on 23rd June 1864. Subsequent purchase of land and construction was fairly rapid, the line opening to traffic on 16th April 1866. In return for 50% of gross takings the Great Eastern Railway provided staff, locomotives and rolling stock.

The Great Eastern Railway was also largely responsible for promotion of the westwards extension from Sutton to Needingworth Junction, near St Ives, in 1876, the opening taking place on 10th May 1878. This date also signalled the official renaming to the Ely & St Ives Railway. The company of that name was eventually bought out by the Great Eastern Railway in 1898.

Details immediately following both the Grouping in 1923 and Nationalisation in 1948 were the same as for the main line, except that the LNER era had seen the withdrawal of passenger services on 2nd February 1931. The final goods trains ran in 1964.

> # G. E. R.
> ---
> # Cambridge

PASSENGER SERVICES

Cambridge to Ely

Details included here refer only to services connecting the two extremities of this section of the main line. Passenger trains heading north from Cambridge would also have included those branching east for the Ipswich line via Newmarket and Bury St Edmunds. The branch service to Fordham and Mildenhall, also heading east, left the main line at Barnwell Junction, while those taking the westerly route at Chesterton Junction could include St Ives, Kettering and March among their destinations. Of all these, the only service which survived after 1970 was that towards Ipswich.

In May 1849 the two cities were connected by six services, five of which stopped at Waterbeach. The increase in the latter half of the nineteenth century was steady, if less than spectacular, and, by 1894, there were 14 daily services. Waterbeach appears to have fallen from grace as only four of these trains deigned to call.

The next 75 years saw surprisingly little advance, with 15 trains in 1929 and only 18 in 1969. Those stopping intermediately at Waterbeach in these years were seven and eight respectively.

However, following privatisation in the mid-1990s, a staggering total of 60 daily trains was provided by the summer of 2005; Waterbeach enjoyed stops by 26 of them. This increase was due to the fact that the line linking the two cities was common to four separately operated longer distance services, two by WAGN and one each by Central and **one**.

Of the two routes converging with the main line just south of Ely, that from the east survived into 2005, while details of the other, from St Ives, are outlined below.

St Ives to Ely.

On a line on which the intermediate stations served only farming communities, the service, of which that for 1882 was typical, was provided to meet local needs. Apart from the first and last trains of the day, which ran daily, there were two more which ran only on Mondays and Thursdays (St. Ives and Ely market days respectively), but on other days of the week, one middle of the day service sufficed.

By the Summer of 1929 there were three daily trains in each direction plus an additional service on Mondays and on Thursdays.

As late as the mid-1930s an early Monday morning goods train included a coach which provided accommodation for drovers heading for St Ives market.

G. E. R.
———
Waterbeach

ELY, SUTTON, and ST. IVES.—G.E.

Fm Yrmth, 105	mrn	mrn	mrn	aft	aft	aft
Ely ......dep	6 10	9 20	9 30	2 5	4 37	7 7
Stretham	6 20	a	9 40	a	a	a
Wilburton ..	6 28	a	9 48	a	a	a
Haddenham	6 36	9 37	10 10	2 20	4 43	7 24
Sutton	6 50	9 42	10 25	2 25	4 58	7 29
Earith Bridge	7 2	a	10 40	a	a	a
Bluntisham..	7 10	9 57	10 53	2 39	5 12	7 44
St. Ives 106	7 20	10 5	11 5	2 47	5 20	7 52

Fm Hntngdn, 106	mrn	mrn	aft	aft	aft
St. Ives ....dep	7 30	1130	1247	3 0	5 30
Bluntisham....	7 38	1139	1255	3 11	5 38
Earith Bridge..	a	1144	a	3 18	a
Sutton	7 53	1155	1 10	3 32	5 51
Haddenham....	7 58	12 1	1 15	3 40	5 58
Wilburton.	a	12 5	a	3 45	a
Stretham.. [106	a	1211	a	3 52	a
Ely 104, 105,	8 15	1220	1 32	4 0	6 15

a Stops when required.

August 1881

March 1909

ELY, SUTTON, and ST. IVES.—Great Eastern.

Miles		Week Days.							Miles		Week Days.						
		mrn	aft		aft	aft					mrn	mrn		aft	aft	aft	
	Ely ....dep	9 25	2 10		4 25	7 10	....	....		St. Ives ....dep	7 30	1135		1250	3 15	5 23	....
2¼	Stretham	9 32	2 16		4 31	7 16	....	....	3¼	Bluntisham	7 38	1143		1258	3 23	5 31	....
4¼	Wilburton	9 38	2 21		4 36	7 21	....	....	5¾	Earith Bridge	7 43	1148	1 3		3 28	5 36	....
5¾	Haddenham	9 42	2 25		4 40	7 25	....	....	10¼	Sutton	7 53	1158	1 13		3 38	5 45	....
7¼	Sutton	9 47	2 30		4 45	7 30	....	....	12	Haddenham	7 58	12 3	1 18		3 43	5 50	....
12	Earith Bridge	9 56	2 39		4 54	7 39	....	....	13	Wilburton..........	8 2	12 7	1 22		3 47	5 54	....
14	Bluntisham	10 2	2 45		5 0	7 45	....	....	15	Stretham ......[301	8 8	1213	1 28		3 53	5 59	....
17¼	St. Ives 299, 562 arr	10 10	2 53		5 8	7 53	....	....	17¼	Ely 294, 298, 300, arr	8 15	1220	1 35		4 0	6 5	....

November 1930

ELY, SUTTON, and ST. IVES.

Miles	Up.	Week Days only.						Miles	Down.	Week Days only.					
		mrn	..	aft	aft	aft	..			mrn		aft	aft	aft	aft
	Ely ....dep	9 45	..	2 0	4 38	6 49	..		St. Ives..........dep	7 19		1215	1245	3 10	5 23
2¼	Stretham	9 52	..	2 7	4 45	6 56	..	3¼	Bluntisham	7 27		1223	1253	3 18	5 31
4¼	Wilburton	9 57	..	2 12	4 50	7 1	..	5¾	Earith Bridge	7 35		1228	1258	3 23	5 36
5¾	Haddenham (Cambs.)..	10 1	..	2 16	4 54	7 5	..	10¼	Sutton	7 49		1237	1 7	3 34	5 47
7¼	Sutton	10 6	..	2 21	4 59	7 11	..	12	Haddenham (Cambs.)	7 59		1242	1 12	3 42	5 52
12	Earith Bridge	1015	..	2 30	5 8	7 20	..	13	Wilburton...........	8 4		1246	1 16	3 47	5 56
14	Bluntisham	1021	..	2 36	5 14	7 26	..	15	Stretham...[880, 881	8 13		1252	1 22	3 53	6 2
17¼	St. Ives 677, 879 arr.	1029	..	2 44	5 22	7 34	..	17¼	Ely 860, 862, 876, arr.	8 21		1258	1 28	3 59	6 11

1. St.Ives to Ely
(Sutton Branch Junction)

I. At the time that this 1888 plan was surveyed, the construction of the new platform, adjacent to the "S" in "Station", was clearly well advanced, although the new footbridge had yet to be put in place.

ST. IVES

1.   We are standing on the up platform around 1930, as a class J17 0-6-0 approaches from the north. A Board of Trade report dated 23rd April 1887 comments on the addition of this platform and the footbridge - previously all March line passenger trains had been handled at the platform on the left. Beneath the footbridge, a notice invites passengers to change for Godmanchester and Huntingdon, whilst on the extreme left of the picture, a smaller sign points out that this is the "Junction for Sutton & Ely line". (Stations UK)

> **Other views of this station can be found in**
> ***Branch Lines around Huntingdon and***
> ***Branch Lines around March.***

2.   Reminding us that the GN & GE Joint line southwards from Doncaster was an important freight route, class K1 2-6-0 no. 62039 curves round into the station with an up goods train around 1960. The line from here to March closed on 4th March 1967, and the station became unstaffed from the same date. (NRS Archive)

3.   The station building stood in the angle of the March and Huntingdon lines. Here it is in the 1960s, with the shadow of the buildings on the western platform beginning to darken the forecourt. The last passenger train to Huntingdon ran in June 1959, and the service to Cambridge lingered on until 3rd October 1970. (J.Watling)

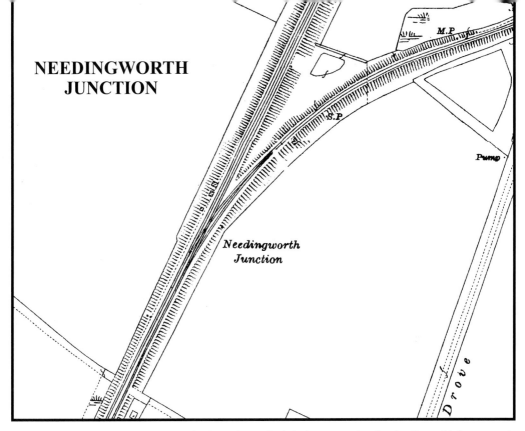

NEEDINGWORTH JUNCTION

Needingworth Junction

II.   This is the junction where the branch to Ely left the somewhat busier line which ran north to March. The rather remote location is shown as it appeared in 1926.

4.   Just under two miles north of St Ives, we find the lonely junction signal box, with the GN & GE Joint line running dead straight into the distance, and the Ely branch curving away to the east. Branch passenger trains have been withdrawn for some 30 years, but there is still double-track access to the line. (NRS Archive)

5.   We are looking along the branch, towards the main line and the signal box, on 6th September 1963. A pump action platelayers' trolley, of the kind beloved by film-makers, stands at the base of the signal. (R.Powell)

6.   Now we climb the steps for a look at the interior of the signal box, again in September 1963. It possessed a 16 lever frame, and the white plates indicate that five of the levers are spare. (R.Powell)

BLUNTISHAM

III.   In common with the other smaller stations on the branch, one double ended siding and a short spur serving the cattle pen were sufficient to handle the demands of the goods traffic. On this 1926 plan the western end of the village appears in the top right hand corner.

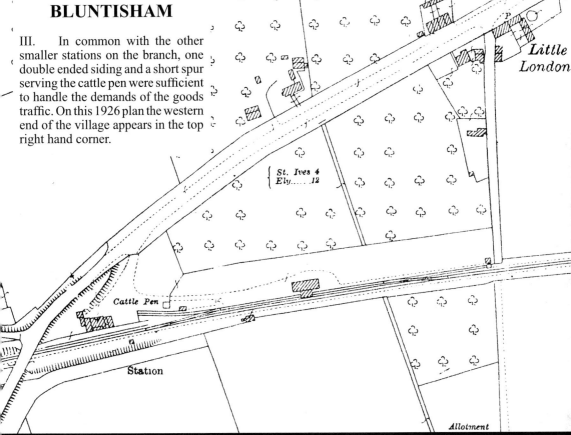

Little London

St. Ives 4
Ely...... 12

Cattle Pen

Station

Allotment

7.   A pile of luggage stands on the platform, but there is no sign of any passengers, as we look eastwards from the road bridge around 1930. Everything is very neat and tidy, with the station name spelt out in white-painted stone on the side of the cutting opposite the main building. The signal box and wooden goods shed flank the running line beyond the platform. Beyond the railway, the church spire indicates that the village is not far away - and as we shall see, this was not the case elsewhere on this branch line.   (Lens of Sutton Collection)

8.	This area suffered badly from flooding during 1947, and the station proved to be a convenient railhead for the Duke and Duchess of Gloucester when they visited the stricken area. The royal visitors' Rolls Royce has drawn up on the platform, clear of the mud, but the motor cycle escort and onlookers in the station yard will certainly need their Wellington boots.
(Cambridgeshire Collection, Cambridge Central Library)

9.	After this excitement, the station settled down to another seventeen years of handling little more than a daily goods train, and the very occasional seaside excursion. The goods train covered the whole length of the line until October 1958, when the section from here to Sutton closed completely. Traffic over the western stub of the line lingered on for a further six years, before being withdrawn from 5th October 1964. Class J15 0-6-0 no. 65477 stands by the disused platform whilst working a goods train during the late 1950s. (D.Lawrence)

10.   The basic amenities of a water closet and wash-house were provided in 1883 at a cost of £35, and from then on the station altered little. As we see here, the structure was intact in August 1967, and in 2005 the exterior was virtually unchanged. By then the station building was a private residence, and, together with the platform and road bridge, it provided perhaps the most complete reminder of the railway. (Railway Record of the British Isles/G.L.Pring)

EAST OF BLUNTISHAM

11.   We catch up with the Duke and Duchess of Gloucester on their 1947 visit, as they return to the train at the east end of the viaduct spanning the River Ouse and surrounding meadows. Behind the train, the viaduct stretches across the flooded countryside, midway between Bluntisham and Earith Bridge stations. Some of the brick piers were still standing into the 21st century. (Cambridgeshire Collection, Cambridge Central Library)

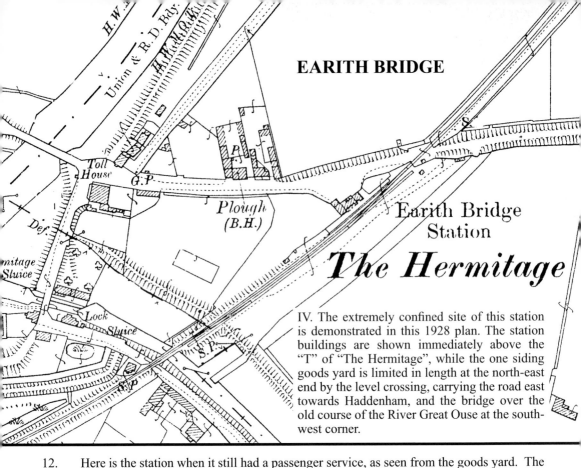

EARITH BRIDGE

Earith Bridge
Station

The Hermitage

IV. The extremely confined site of this station is demonstrated in this 1928 plan. The station buildings are shown immediately above the "T" of "The Hermitage", while the one siding goods yard is limited in length at the north-east end by the level crossing, carrying the road east towards Haddenham, and the bridge over the old course of the River Great Ouse at the south-west corner.

12.　　Here is the station when it still had a passenger service, as seen from the goods yard. The signal box, at the south end of the platform, was abolished in 1932. (Cambridgeshire Collection, Cambridge Central Library)

13.   Now we are looking along the track towards Ely, with three members of the station staff standing on the wooden platform. Staffing levels on the line were reduced in December 1922, when conductor-guard working was introduced in an attempt to cut operating costs. As a result the booking offices at all the intermediate stations except Sutton and Haddenham were closed, and the guard issued tickets on the train. (A. Ingram)

14.   Surprisingly, the station building is receiving considerable attention in 1937, six years after the end of passenger services. Replacement slates have been fitted on the roof, while the brickwork on the wall of the lock-up shed has been renewed. At the far end of the platform, two workmen contemplate scaling the ladder which is propped up against the stationmaster's house. The platform facing has been reinforced with lengths of old rail, whilst the southern end of the platform has been shortened by a few yards. (Stations UK)

15.   Here is the road approach to the station building, during the 1950s. A post box remains, set in the wall of the booking office, so the long-closed station continues to provide a service to the community. The single-storey part of the stationmaster's house looks none too safe, possibly as a result of the same subsidence that led to the reduction in platform length. (B.Nunns/A.Mott)

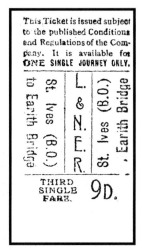

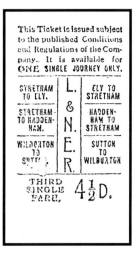

16.   During the Summer of 1955, a shirt sleeved railwayman waits by the level crossing gates at the north end of the station, as class J17 0-6-0 no. 65565 rolls in with a lightweight goods train. Following the passenger closure, the daily goods train was scheduled to run from Ely to St Ives in the morning, returning eastwards during the afternoon.   Times varied, but this pattern was maintained right up until 1958. (Stations UK)

17.   To the south of the station, a bridge carried the line over the Old West River, adjacent to another level crossing. With the railings of the river bridge on the right, a lorry rumbles over the crossing on 29th November 1961, representing the future of freight transport in the Fens. The gatehouse was still there in 2005, as were the railings and bridge abutment. However, across the river, the station site had been excavated to form a marina, supplementing the complex of waterways in the vicinity. (J.H.Meredith)

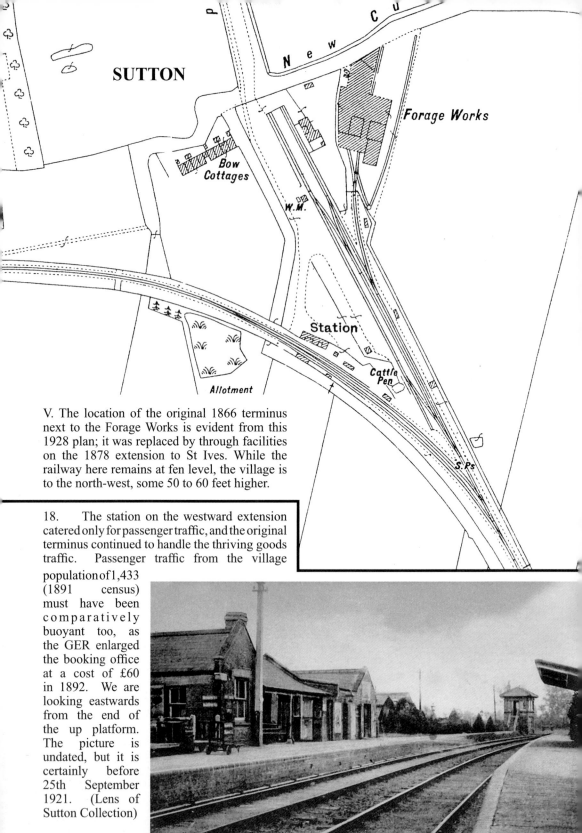

SUTTON

Forage Works

Bow
Cottages

W.M.

Station

Cattle
Pen

Allotment

S.Ps

V. The location of the original 1866 terminus next to the Forage Works is evident from this 1928 plan; it was replaced by through facilities on the 1878 extension to St Ives. While the railway here remains at fen level, the village is to the north-west, some 50 to 60 feet higher.

18.   The station on the westward extension catered only for passenger traffic, and the original terminus continued to handle the thriving goods traffic.   Passenger traffic from the village population of 1,433 (1891 census) must have been comparatively buoyant too, as the GER enlarged the booking office at a cost of £60 in 1892. We are looking eastwards from the end of the up platform. The picture is undated, but it is certainly before 25th September 1921. (Lens of Sutton Collection)

19.   A fire was discovered in the station building during the early hours of Sunday 25th September 1921, and a contemporary report in the local newspaper tells how the local fire brigade was called to the scene, only to run out of water. The telegraphist at the village Post Office was roused from his slumber, and he in turn contacted the GER fire brigade at Cambridge. They received the call at 4.30 a.m., and having "chartered a special train for their (fire) engine" arrived on the scene at 6.50 a.m. to find the fire still raging. Faintly farcical as this might appear in our age of instant communications, it is nonetheless a reminder of just how isolated rural communities could be. When the flames were eventually extinguished, the roof had collapsed, leaving just the walls and chimney stack standing. All records and bank notes had been destroyed, but some silver coins, part of the works of the clock and the frame of the automatic chocolate machine were reportedly found in the ashes. Here is the scene after the blaze, as depicted in the "Ely Standard". (Cambridgeshire Collection, Cambridge Central Library)

20.   The station was rebuilt at a cost of £398.15.0 after the fire, but was to see less than a decade of passenger use. Although the single storey replacement building was at first glance similar, a comparison between this 1955 view and picture 18 will reveal the differences. By a strange coincidence, this building too was gutted by fire during the mid-1960s. The distant church emphasises the difference in levels between the village and the railway. (Stations UK)

21.   We are standing at the west end of the loop on a sunny 28th July 1961. To the left of the signal box, a smudge of smoke reveals that a locomotive is shunting on the line to the goods station. (R.Powell)

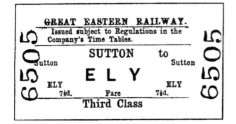

22.   On the same day, a class J17 0-6-0 runs round a handful of wagons, before backing them down the line to the goods station. Working timetables between 1934 and 1949 show that goods traffic on the eastern section justified an afternoon train to Ely in addition to the through working to and from St Ives, but this was discontinued in 1950. Between 1947 and 1949 the branch was used by two daily brick trains running from Fletton to Norwich, presumably in connection with post-war rebuilding work. (R.Powell)

23.   The signalbox here, as at the other locations on the western extension, was of the standard Saxby and Farmer design, quite unlike those found elsewhere on the Great Eastern system. It was the only one on the line to survive after 1932, and the station remained fully signalled until the goods service was withdrawn on 13th July 1964. Now it waits for the demolition men on 7th August 1964. (R.Powell)

SUTTON (ORIGINAL STATION)

24.   From 1902 Drakes Forage Works were served by this siding next to the 1866 station.   The neighbours were not happy – Mr Sheard of Sutton is recorded as complaining about the smells in the early days.   Nonetheless the works generated regular traffic for the railway until the private siding agreement was terminated from 31st August 1934.
(Cambridgeshire Collection, Cambridge Central Library)

(lower left) 25. On another occasion, a slightly wider viewpoint captures the charming scruffiness of the area. Two employees pause from their labours beside an old boiler, dumped between the tracks that converge on a wagon turntable. The site was taken over by coal merchants Coote and Warren by a private siding agreement dated 9th December 1936, and this remained in force until the final closure. (Cambridgeshire Collection, Cambridge Central Library)

26. The shunt arm on the signal reveals that class J17 0-6-0 no. 65578 is propelling some wagons down to the goods station on 28th July 1961. We are standing between the tracks which lead round to the second station. (R.Powell)

27. The original station building was similar to those at Bluntisham, Earith Bridge and Haddenham, consisting of a two-storey station master's house adjoining the single-storey offices. It ceased to handle passengers in May 1878, but its survival as a goods station for another 86 years probably justified the Great Eastern's expenditure of £25 on sinking a well in 1875. We are standing on the goods platform on 6th August 1967, looking across the overgrown wilderness where the rails once were. By 2005 little trace remained of either station. (Railway Record of the British Isles/G.L.Pring)

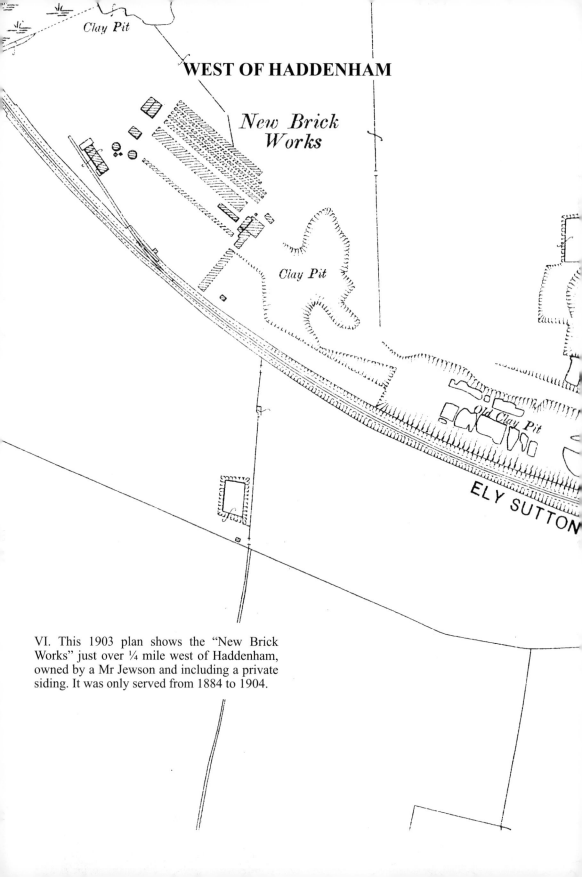

Clay Pit

WEST OF HADDENHAM

*New Brick
Works*

Clay Pit

Old Clay Pit

ELY SUTTON

VI. This 1903 plan shows the "New Brick Works" just over ¼ mile west of Haddenham, owned by a Mr Jewson and including a private siding. It was only served from 1884 to 1904.

HADDENHAM

VII. By contrast, a continuation south-eastwards of plan VI shows another similar establishment, latterly owned by the Isle of Ely Brickworks which appears to have survived into the 1950s. The premises were served by a private siding connection from the goods yard. Haddenham was the largest community on the line at opening (pop.2055 in 1871); the station was located at the northern extremity of the village, but, as in the case of Sutton, at a somewhat lower level.

Clay Pit

E. R.

S.P.   S.P.   *Cattle Pen*   M.P

· IVES BRANCH   S.P.   S.B.

Station

ay Pit

Goods Shed

L.B   P *Railway*
   W *Hotel*

Clay Pit

P

Brick & Til
Works

28.   A group of people pose for the photographer in front of the station building during the late nineteenth century, whilst the station master's family are leaning from the upstairs window, determined to get in on the act. Five of the people appear to be uniformed railway staff, and it is arguable whether the others are genuine passengers, or simply villagers brought in by the photographer to enliven the scene. Either way, it is a valuable record, for a new house was built for the stationmaster in 1900, and the old one was demolished.
(Cambridgeshire Collection, Cambridge Central Library)

29.   Looking east from the road bridge in 1952, we can see that the single-storey part of the building remained very much in its original form, although expenditure of £150 had been authorised on new booking office facilities in 1900. A retaining wall and various huts have replaced the house. There are plenty of wagons in the sidings, and the chimney of the brickworks looks down on the area. (Stations UK)

30.   A grimy class J17 0-6-0 stands at the platform during the late 1950s. The nameboard reads "Haddenham Cambs": the LNER added the county suffix to prevent any possible confusion, however unlikely, with Haddenham in Buckinghamshire. Stations on the branch handled a large quantity of fruit and vegetables grown in the surrounding area, and traffic was not confined to the traditional "coal inwards and sugar beet outwards" of so many East Anglian country stations at this time. (I.C.Allen / The Transport Treasury)

31.   The extremities of half forgotten sidings could provide scenes of great atmosphere. Here is the goods shed on 31st July 1961- the grass suggests that nothing has entered it for ages, but who knows what might be lurking in the darkness beyond the imposing barred gate? Next door, the "Railway Hotel" declares allegiance to the products of Morgans Brewery in distant Norwich, an historic business that was in its last year of independence. (J.Watling)

G. E. R.
Haddenham

32.   The 1900 stationmaster's house overlooks the area as we look towards Sutton on 22ⁿᵈ July 1964. Now everything is still, as the goods service had been withdrawn earlier in the month. The long down siding, parallel to the running line, has already been removed, and the remaining tracks will follow. (R.Powell)

33.   We take a final look eastwards along the platform on 6th August 1967, after the tracks were lifted. The long-lived running-in board has gone at last, but a lamp and, remarkably, the "You may TELEPHONE from here" sign still cling tenaciously to the building. In later years the site was taken over by a light industrial complex. Pleasingly, the stationmaster's house was incorporated in the new development, and was still instantly recognisable in 2005. (Railway Record of the British Isles/ G.L.Pring)

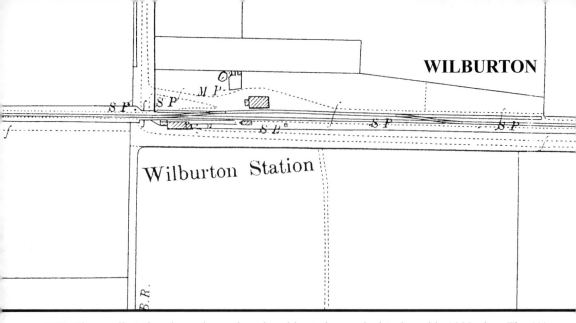

VIII. The small station theme is continued at this station as depicted on this 1928 plan. The 1½ mile approach from the village with a population of barely 550, was by a rather tortuous, exposed route.

34.   The station buildings here were fairly small, but included a booking office, waiting room and accommodation for the stationmaster. Following complaints from passengers, these were supplemented in 1904 by the provision of a ladies toilet. As at the other stations, the running-in board survives in this picture dated 21st May 1962. This was unusual, as the authorities normally removed them promptly after closure. It has been suggested, quite logically, that they may have remained to guide passengers on the seaside excursions that continued to run, once or twice a year, until 1958. (J.Watling)

35.   The full extent of the platform and buildings can be seen as we look west from the goods yard to the station on 22nd July 1964. A noteworthy feature is the angle of the canopy, rising sharply away from the building to allow clearance for the passing trains. This scene had probably changed little over nearly a century. (R.Powell)

36.   Now we turn to look eastwards on the same day. The goods shed, served by a double-ended siding, is the only building to be seen, and dominates the landscape as the line continues dead straight across the flat countryside towards Stretham. (R.Powell)

37.   Here is the station building from the south-west later in the decade. British Railways poster boards attached to the fencing and the western wall provide information for potential rail users. (Cambridgeshire Collection, Cambridge Central Library)

38.   As we move round to the west of the station, we find that the level crossing gates, awning and goods shed are still in place. The only thing missing is the track! In 2005 a new residence had been built on the site, and "Station Cottages" further down the road towards Grunty Fen provided the only major clue that the trains once ran nearby. (Cambridgeshire Collection, Cambridge Central Library)

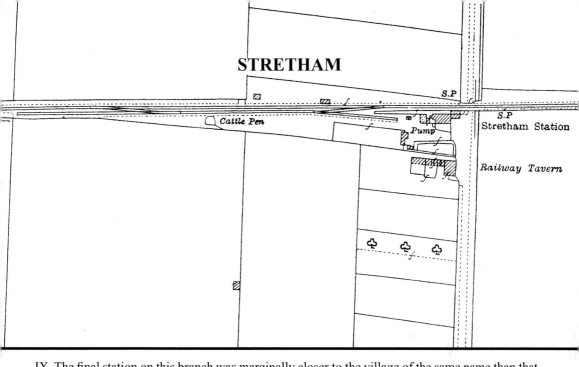

STRETHAM

Cattle Pen

S.P

S.P
Stretham Station

Pump

Railway Tavern

IX. The final station on this branch was marginally closer to the village of the same name than that at Wilburton, but not close enough to make the effort to get to it any less attractive with the main road from Cambridge to Ely running through the village centre. By the time of this 1926 map, the local motor bus was much more appealing.

39.   The guard prepares to close the level crossing gates behind the goods train, which has dropped off a couple of wagons as it makes its way back to Ely on 28th July 1961. (R.Powell)

40.   Two signs advise passers-by that they may use the telephone, whilst posters tell them the name of the stationmaster, and remind them that the station is open for goods and parcels traffic. An oil lamp guards the entrance to the platform, and the station name is prominently displayed. There is little to indicate that it is 21st May 1962, and that the station has been closed to passengers for over thirty years. (J.Watling)

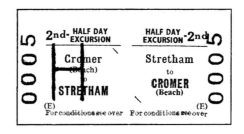

41.   The simple buildings here were similar to those at Wilburton, but the height of the booking office was greater, thus enabling the canopy to project at a more conventional 90°. Since the signal box was abolished in 1932, the points giving access to the goods siding had been controlled by the lever emerging from the grass on the right of the picture. We are looking in the direction of Ely on 22nd July 1964. (R.Powell)

42.   The southern aspect of the station, seen here on 6th August 1967, emphasises just how small the flat roofed office building was, and the adjoining house appears quite substantial by comparison. By 2005 the station house had been demolished, but the smaller building was still there, complete with its awning. (Railway Record of the British Isles/G.L.Pring)

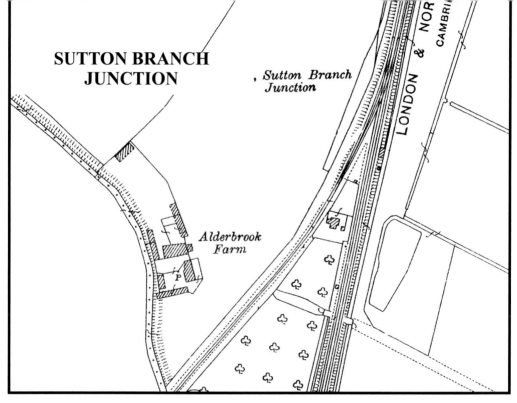

SUTTON BRANCH
JUNCTION

*, Sutton Branch
Junction*

*Alderbrook
Farm*

X. The arrangement shown in this 1926 plan changed dramatically following the withdrawal of the branch passenger service. In July 1932 the junction was eliminated, the signal box closed and all trains to and from the branch were routed via a new down reception line to Ely station.

43.   We are looking back from the brake van of the Sutton goods train, along the branch towards the junction, on 28th July 1961. Conveniently for the photographer, a class J20 0-6-0 steams past on the main line, heading for Ely. Within a year, steam engines would have disappeared from most of East Anglia. (R.Powell)

44.　　By 26th April 1969 the branch had been lifted to within a few yards of the junction, and here we see the final short stub curving away to the west, before petering out in the undergrowth. The "down independent line" connects with the main line by the signal. We are looking out of the window of a train bound for Cambridge, and we too will now head for the University city. From here we will make our way back to Ely along the busy main line – a contrast from the sleepy branch line that has brought us from St Ives. (Railway Record of the British Isles/G.L.Pring)

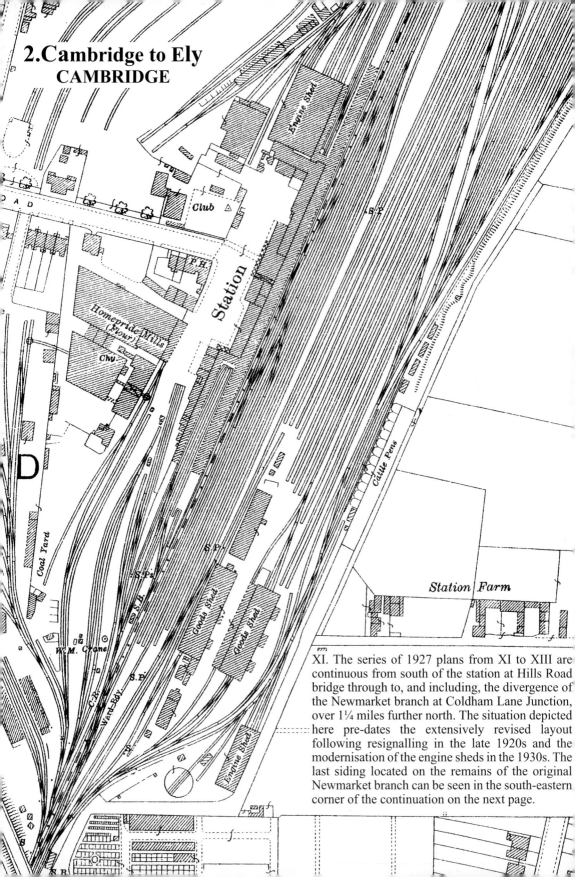

2. Cambridge to Ely
CAMBRIDGE

Engine Shed

Club

Station

P.H.

Homepride Mills
(Flour)

Chy.

S.P.

S.P.

D

Coal Yard

S.Ps.

S.B.

Goods Shed

Goods Shed

S.P.

W.M. Crane

C.B.

Want.Bdy.

S.P.

Engine Shed

Cattle Pens

Station Farm

XI. The series of 1927 plans from XI to XIII are continuous from south of the station at Hills Road bridge through to, and including, the divergence of the Newmarket branch at Coldham Lane Junction, over 1¼ miles further north. The situation depicted here pre-dates the extensively revised layout following resignalling in the late 1920s and the modernisation of the engine sheds in the 1930s. The last siding located on the remains of the original Newmarket branch can be seen in the south-eastern corner of the continuation on the next page.

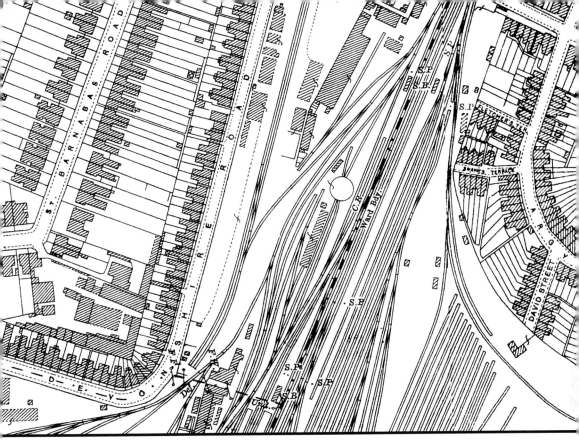

45.   The station area is bounded by the bridges carrying Hills Road at the south end and Mill Road to the north. This early photograph gives us a rare sight of the signal box that stood in the shadow of Hills Road between 1883 and 1926. The road curves round past the cattle pens, dating from 1885, towards the GER goods shed on the right. (Cambridgeshire Collection, Cambridge Central Library)

46.   Horse drawn transport is much in evidence in front of the impressive façade of the station. It is often said that the university authorities were strongly opposed to the railway but in reality there was probably no more than an understandable wariness towards the brash new means of transport. Certainly there was enough mutual respect to justify the coats of arms of the colleges being incorporated into the frontage of the new station, and we can see these here in the circular designs between the arches. (J.Watling collection)

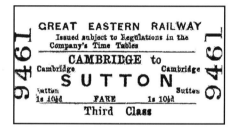

47.   The Great Northern Railway possessed its own station building, immediately to the south of the Great Eastern one. In the days before World War 1, a group of cabbies line up in orderly fashion waiting for business outside the GNR building. No doubt they are hoping for generous tips from students returning to the colleges, which were, without exception, some distance from the railway. The building remained in railway use in 2005, and the GNR architectural style was still instantly recognisable. (Cambridgeshire Collection, Cambridge Central Library)

48.   Now we join a bowler-hatted gentleman at the north end of the platform, as he looks towards the signal box and the lines disappearing through the distant Mill Road bridge. The signal box stood on this site from 1896, when the platform was lengthened, until 1926, when a replacement was constructed some distance to the north. (J.Watling collection)

49.   The station layout has provided various operating eccentricities over the years. Not least of these was the junction of the line to Newmarket, which diverged from the main line alongside the platform and curved sharply eastwards, crossing at least five other tracks in the process. Here is the junction on 27th August 1911, some fifteen years after the Newmarket line junction had been moved north to Coldham Lane. Part of the old route remained in use as a siding, and it was eventually lifted during the late 1920s, enabling the goods facilities on the east side of the main line to be extended and the surplus land to be sold for £10,000. (J.Watling collection)

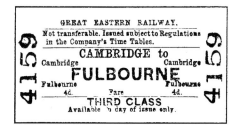

GREAT EASTERN RAILWAY.

4159

Not transferable. Issued subject to Regulations in the Company's Time Tables.

CAMBRIDGE to

Cambridge   Cambridge

FULBOURNE

Fulbourne   Fulbourne
4d.   Fare   4d.

THIRD CLASS
Available n day of issue only.

4159

50. Further operating difficulties were caused by the fact that the main platform comprised one continuous face, despite Board of Trade recommendations in 1885 and 1897 that a new up platform should be built. A central signalbox helped to regulate the traffic, and is seen here overlooking the scissors crossover, which enables trains to use both the south and north ends of the platform simultaneously. (Lens of Sutton Collection)

51. We are looking north in Great Eastern days, with the scissors crossover prominent in the foreground. As we saw in picture 49, the GER was always ready to bring in revenue from advertising, and even the canopy supports are being used to highlight the virtues of Stephens Gum. (J.Watling collection)

52.　　A general view of the station during the GER era again emphasises the single main platform, with a train waiting in one of the south end bays. Next to the locomotive on the left is a smaller double-sided bay platform, which appeared on plans as late as 1927. A flat truck was stabled in this platform, carrying a horse-drawn Merryweather fire engine, ready to be sent out as necessary or unloaded quickly if there was a local emergency. No doubt the brigade would have set out from here in their bid to save Sutton station in 1921. (J.Watling collection)

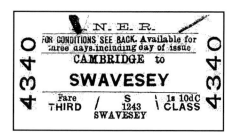

53.   Foster's granary dominated the land to the west of the station, and provides a unique vantage point for the next two photographs, which date from the late 1920s. Firstly we look southwards over a busy goods yard towards Hills Road bridge. Two passenger trains are waiting to leave the south end bay platforms: another engine stands by the resited Cambridge South signal box, and a fourth locomotive stands in the goods yard to the right.
(Cambridgeshire Collection, Cambridge Central Library).

54.   We turn to look westwards, with the houses on Hills Road bordering the GNR goods yard. Coal appears to be the major traffic, with a preponderance of private owner wagons belonging to the local coal merchants, Austin & Co. However, other traffic is catered for by the cattle pens and substantial goods shed. The yard was closed from 31st January 1966, and, perhaps surprisingly, the area remained undeveloped in 2005, although used for car parking.
(Cambridgeshire Collection, Cambridge Central Library)

55.   The engine shed was next to the north end bay platform, and only a low wall separated the engines from the waiting passengers. These two ladies are still smiling despite the rain-soaked platform beneath their feet and the sizzling monsters behind them. (Cambridgeshire Collection, Cambridge Central Library)

56.   Facilities for dealing with engines had developed piecemeal over the years, and the whole motive power depot was thoroughly modernised during the early 1930s. Seen from the new mechanical coaling plant in 1934, a class D13 4-4-0 makes use of the equally new 70' turntable. The building to the left is the lifting shop, and the District Engineer's office stands behind the lines of coal wagons. (A.Garraway)

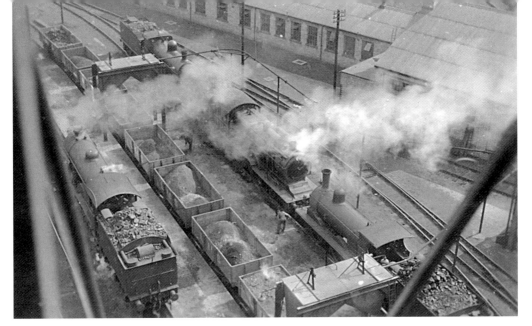

57.   On the same occasion, drifting smoke from four steam engines does little to obscure the view from the dizzy heights of the coaling tower. The locomotive shed is in the background, whilst the sand hoppers and wagons of ash from the engines are prominent. An ex-GNR locomotive combines with three ex-GER engines to illustrate the cosmopolitan nature of the shed. (A.Garraway)

58.   Following a meeting of GER and GNR officials in 1910 it was agreed to make economies by sharing a common booking office and parcels office. Some forty years later, this scene greeted the intending passenger. The booking office windows are set in the wood panelling to the left, with queue barriers in front. Folding metal gates lead through to the platforms, while the train departures board and enquiry office provide information. In 2005 the scene was very different following successive rebuildings, but the pillars remained as a link with the past, amongst the TV screens and retail outlets. (Cambridgeshire Collection, Cambridge Central Library)

59.　　A class E4 2-4-0 is dwarfed by the north end signals during the late 1950s. These signals had been installed as part of a major resignalling scheme in 1925/6, when two new signalboxes replaced the five older ones that had previously been needed. In the distance, Mill Road bridge provides a link with picture 48, while it is reasonable to suggest that the water crane on the right is common to both views. (G.Powell / GERS collection)

60.　　The exterior of the station is still instantly recognisable around 1960, although many of the archways have been glazed and an awning protects the entrance from the elements. A splendid selection of contemporary motor cars has replaced the horse drawn vehicles that we saw earlier. Back in 1858 omnibuses had been charged 5/6d per week to use the forecourt, whilst cabs paid 2/6d weekly, and between 1880 and 1914 the transport interest here was increased by the presence of the horse-drawn tramcars of the Cambridge Street Tramways Company. (NRS Archive)

61.   Class J17 0-6-0 no.65505 takes the goods lines with a southbound freight train during the 1950s, and is approaching Hills Road bridge past the cattle pens. The water tank of the GNR loco shed is to the right of the engine, and the gable of the GER goods shed on the extreme left. (S.V.Blencowe Collection)

62.   The goods shed features again, as we look north along the yard and through the station from Hills Road bridge during the early 1960s. (NRS Archive)

63.   Mill Road bridge provides a similar panorama, this time looking south, at much the same time. The goods lines, avoiding the station, provide a clear path between the stabled coaches and wagons, whilst a number of steam engines stand to the north of the shed. A Sentinel steam

shunter, one of two allocated to Cambridge Engineer's Department, is standing to the right of the signal box. The extent to which the railway expanded to the east of the main line is apparent. (R.S.Carpenter)

64.   Class J19 0-6-0 no. 64656 simmers in the shed yard, again around 1960. By this time, engines working in from the Bletchley line were serviced at the GER shed, and the LMS tender on the right suggests one such visitor. The LNWR shed to the south of Hills Road was no longer used, although the building was still standing.   (NRS Archive)

G. E. R.
———
From_____
TO
CAMBRIDGE

65.   A number of LMS designed Ivatt 2-6-0s were allocated here soon after nationalisation, ensuring that the cosmopolitan atmosphere remained until the end of steam. One of these engines, no. 46400, stands outside the shed with class B1 4-6-0 no. 61363 on June 11th 1962, just a few days before the last steam locos were transferred away. (R.J.Adderson)

66.   The redundant coaling tower was felled by explosive charges during the Summer of 1967. After the dust had settled, a group of onlookers survey the toppled giant. (R.F.Bonny)

67.   We are standing beside the down goods line on 26th October 1969, looking south through Mill Road bridge with Mill Road Junction signalbox to the right. The bridge replaced a level crossing around 1889, and at the same time the signal box succeeded an earlier structure to the south of the road on the up side of the line. (Railway Record of the British Isles/G.L.Pring)

68.　　After steam traction finished, part of the engine shed yard remained in use as a stabling point for diesel locomotives. With Cambridge North signal box beyond, no. 47115 waits in the sidings between turns on 15th October 1982. (D.C.Pearce)

69.　　This aerial view shows just how much the railway presence had contracted by the 1980s. The station building remains an unmistakable feature in the top right hand corner, but the sidings to the east of the main line are much reduced. The rectangular piece of land bounded by Station Road, Tenison Road and Devonshire Road is largely given over to car parking, whilst the timber yard which had long existed in uneasy proximity to the steam shed, has expanded to cover the northern part of the site. (Ridgeons Ltd)

70.   Further changes came in 1983, when the track layout was rationalised and control of the signalling passed to a modern power box to the south-west of the station. This new building is prominent as a class 37 stands at the platform with a parcels train on 12th June 1982, partly obscuring Cambridge South signal box. (R.Powell)

71.   Over the years, the line through here has been a useful diversionary route when the East Coast main line has been blocked, and local enthusiasts from the 1950s and 1960s have fond memories of Gresley pacifics and Deltics passing through on express trains. In more recent times, a diverted HST set heads south through the station on 6th April 1986. (D.C.Pearce)

72.   Electric services on the Liverpool Street route began in May 1987, and were extended north to Ely and Kings Lynn in 1992. No 305519, of a design dating back to 1960, has arrived from Liverpool Street on 15th June 1988, as 86223 Norwich Union runs past. The electric loco is about to replace a class 47 on an up express from Kings Lynn for the electrified stage of the journey. (R.J.Adderson)

73.   No 31250 trundles south through the station with a long engineers' train on 5th February 1993. It is passing under the recently constructed pedestrian and cycle bridge, which spans the tracks through the station. (H.P.White / A.Mott collection)

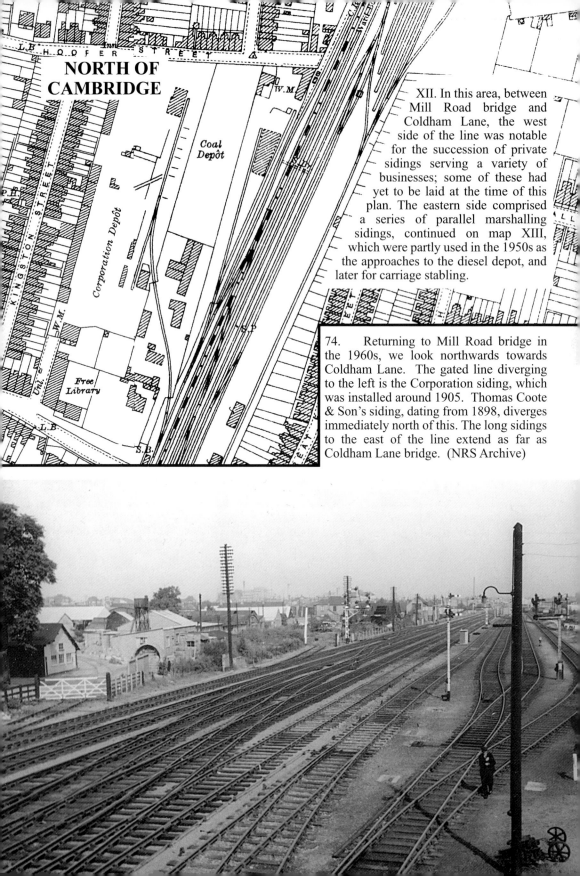

XII. In this area, between Mill Road bridge and Coldham Lane, the west side of the line was notable for the succession of private sidings serving a variety of businesses; some of these had yet to be laid at the time of this plan. The eastern side comprised a series of parallel marshalling sidings, continued on map XIII, which were partly used in the 1950s as the approaches to the diesel depot, and later for carriage stabling.

74.	Returning to Mill Road bridge in the 1960s, we look northwards towards Coldham Lane. The gated line diverging to the left is the Corporation siding, which was installed around 1905. Thomas Coote & Son's siding, dating from 1898, diverges immediately north of this. The long sidings to the east of the line extend as far as Coldham Lane bridge. (NRS Archive)

75.	Trains from the Kettering line (via Huntingdon) brought Midland Railway locomotives to Cambridge on a regular basis. 0-6-0 no. 3195 heads one such train past the entrance to the Corporation siding on 8th March 1938. (P.D.Orton)

76.	In post-war years scrap metal firms occupied the Thomas Coote premises. Two steam locomotives, which had previously operated the Burwell tramway, await their fate here during the early 1960s. (C.Fisher)

77.   Continuing northwards we come to a third private siding. This one served the Cambridge & District Co-op, and was built in accordance with an agreement dated 20th March 1929. The sidings were extended in later years, and the tracks were still in place on 29th April 1984. (R.Powell)

78.   Major changes took place here in the mid-1890s, with the construction of the new line to Newmarket. This branched off in a north-easterly direction and curved sharply round to join the old alignment, thus eliminating the awkward junction at Cambridge station. In connection with this work, the level crossing was replaced by a bridge. The contract was awarded to Holme & King for the not inconsiderable sum of £13,997 on 7th May 1895. Here we see work progressing on the new bridge, with a cart held up at the level crossing gates to the right.
(Cambridgeshire Collection, Cambridge Central Library)

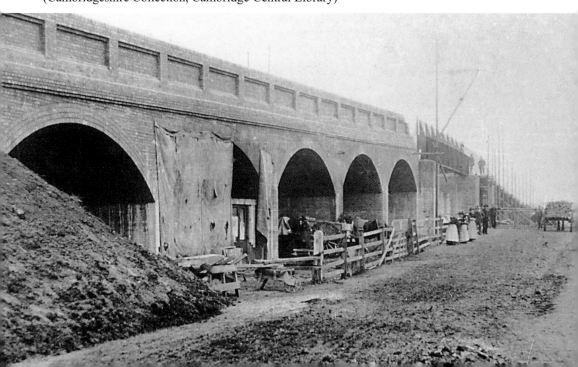

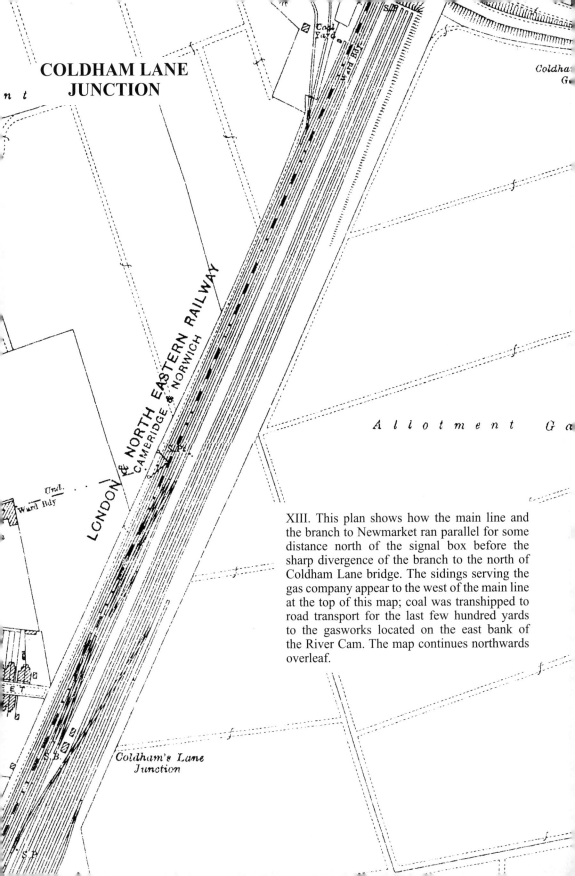

COLDHAM LANE
JUNCTION

LONDON & NORTH EASTERN RAILWAY
CAMBRIDGE & NORWICH

Allotment Ga

XIII. This plan shows how the main line and
the branch to Newmarket ran parallel for some
distance north of the signal box before the
sharp divergence of the branch to the north of
Coldham Lane bridge. The sidings serving the
gas company appear to the west of the main line
at the top of this map; coal was transhipped to
road transport for the last few hundred yards
to the gasworks located on the east bank of
the River Cam. The map continues northwards
overleaf.

*Coldham's Lane
Junction*

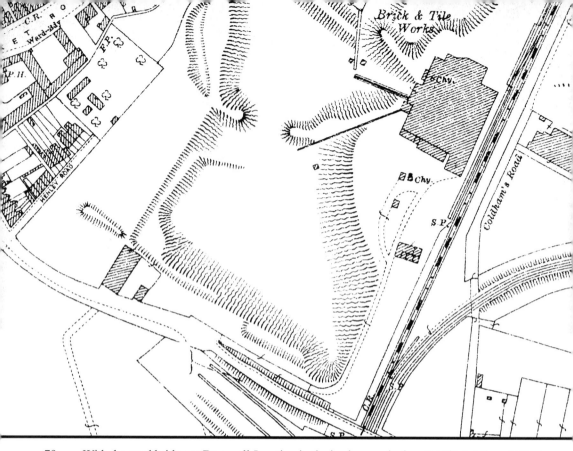

79.   With the road bridge at Barnwell Junction in the background, class D16/3 4-4-0 no. 62618 heads a stopping train southwards towards Coldham Lane Junction during the late 1950s. The private sidings on the left were provided for Watts & Sons, local timber merchants, in 1880. (G.L.Kenworthy collection)

80.　During the late 1950s a diesel depot was built on the site of the sidings to the east of the main line. Two railbuses, the nearer of which is E79961, stand inside the new depot during the early 1960s. The cleanliness of the area provides a dramatic contrast with the working conditions at the old steam shed. (NRS Archive)

81.　The brand new diesel depot dominates the east side of the line, as we look southwards from the road bridge during the early 1960s. By contrast, the roof and chimney pots belong to the original level crossing keeper's cottage. The down loop joins the main line here, but not before providing access to yet more private sidings. Beyond the signal we can make out the junction with a line which served Cadbury & Fry (later Cadbury Schweppes Ltd) between 1959 and 1971, whilst the points at the very end of the loop lead to the gasworks siding. (NRS Archive)

82.   Gas lighting came to Cambridge in the 1830s and the 1861 GER minutes record the construction of a siding to serve the gas works at a cost of £140. The gas company, it was emphasised, would pay the bill. Further extensions and alterations took place before the agreement was terminated in June 1969. A vertical boilered Sentinel locomotive, no.8024, came here new in 1929 and pottered around the site until rail traffic ceased forty years later. It was well turned-out when photographed on 15th October 1960; it could still be seen in 2005 looking just as smart, and in working order, at a preservation site in Preston Docks. (Industrial Railway Society, John Hill Collection)

Other views of this area can be found in
Branch Lines around Huntingdon.

83.   The signal box was opened on 16th May 1896 in connection with the new line towards Newmarket. It gained greater importance with the construction of the diesel depot, and was extended with a 101-lever frame in March 1959. The fresh brickwork of the extension is still prominent on 17th September 1978, some four years before the box was abolished as the result of a major resignalling scheme. (R.Powell)

84.   The Newmarket line curves away to the north-east as a diesel unit heads towards the junction forming a service from Peterborough on 15th October 1982. Watts' sidings have disappeared under the light industrial units that crowd in to the west of the main line, almost all the way back to the distant road bridge at Barnwell Junction. (D.C.Pearce)

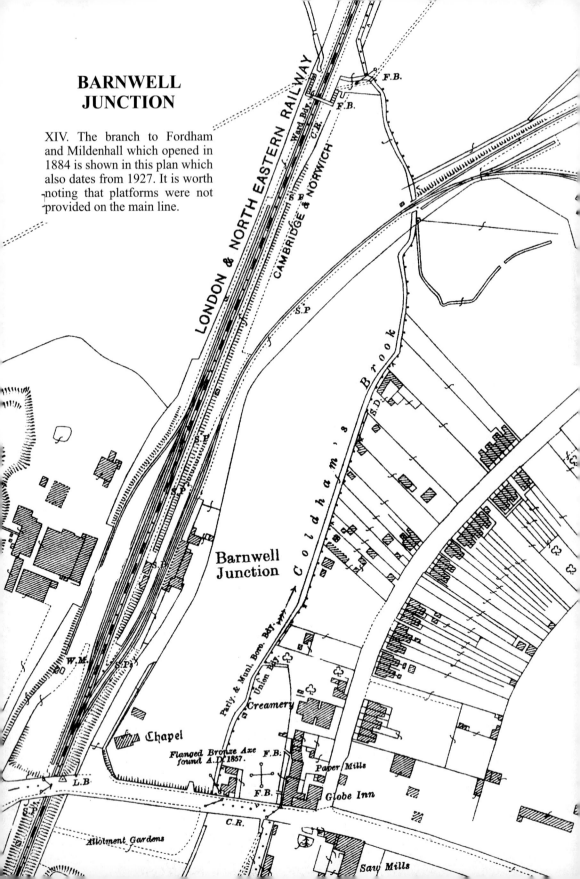

BARNWELL JUNCTION

XIV. The branch to Fordham and Mildenhall which opened in 1884 is shown in this plan which also dates from 1927. It is worth noting that platforms were not provided on the main line.

Barnwell
Junction

LONDON & NORTH EASTERN RAILWAY

CAMBRIDGE & NORWICH

Coldham's Brook

F.B.

F.B.

Creamery

Chapel

Flanged Bronze Axe found A.D. 1857

Paper Mills

Globe Inn

Saw Mills

Allotment Gardens

85.   Class J15 0-6-0 no. 65460 stands in the station with a privately chartered train from Mildenhall on 14th June 1962, just two days before the branch passenger service was withdrawn. (R.J.Adderson collection)

86.   We are looking north past the junction on 20th March 1966. The goods yard is still in use at this time, but would close later in the year, on 31st October. On the far side of the main line a single track still runs through the station to serve the nearby oil depot. (Railway Record of the British Isles/G.L.Pring)

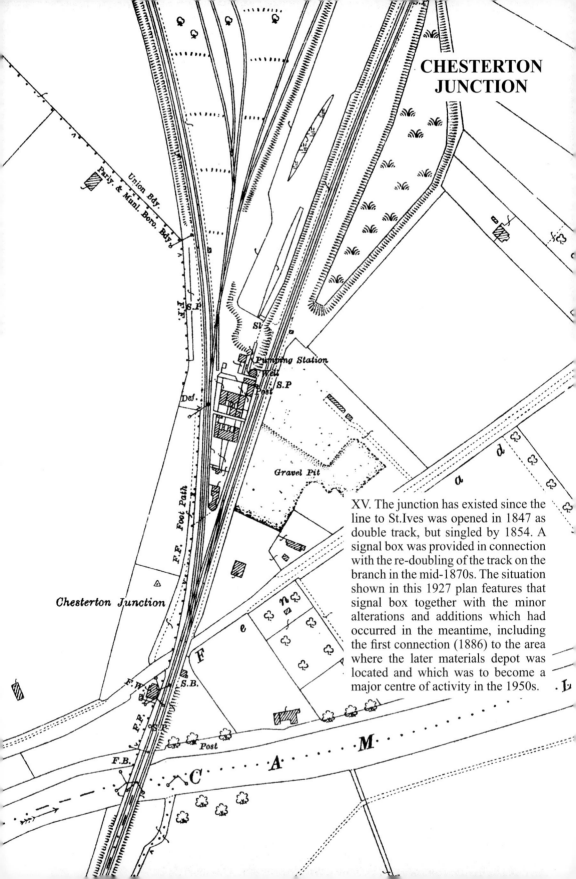

CHESTERTON JUNCTION

Union Bdy.

Parly. & Munl. Boro. Bdy.

F.P. S.P.

Sl.

Pumping Station

Well S.P.

Post

Def.

Gravel Pit

F.P. Foot Path

Chesterton Junction

F

F.W. S.B.

F.P. S.P.

Post

F.B. C A M

XV. The junction has existed since the line to St.Ives was opened in 1847 as double track, but singled by 1854. A signal box was provided in connection with the re-doubling of the track on the branch in the mid-1870s. The situation shown in this 1927 plan features that signal box together with the minor alterations and additions which had occurred in the meantime, including the first connection (1886) to the area where the later materials depot was located and which was to become a major centre of activity in the 1950s.

87.   A somewhat neglected looking group of sidings fills the triangle between the St Ives branch in the foreground, and the main line, whose presence is betrayed by a signal behind the trees to the right. Piles of rail chairs and other materials lying around suggest that the permanent way department was making use of the area when this picture was taken in 1911.
(HMRS H.F. Hilton Collection)

88.   A new bridge was built to span the Cam in 1931, and was the third one on this site. The steelwork was erected on staging to the east of the line, and when complete, the old wrought iron bridge was rolled out to the down side of the line, and the new structure rolled into position. Here we see the operation in progress, with a crowd of onlookers taking a keen interest in proceedings.
(Cambridgeshire Collection, Cambridge Central Library)

89.   With the River Cam in the foreground, class O1 2-8-0 no. 63890 heads a down goods train towards the bridge on 13th February 1960. The train is on an embankment, which had been constructed as part of the 1931 improvements to replace six 10' long approach spans to the south of the bridge. At the same time, another 40' embankment replaced three further spans at the north end of the bridge. (NRS Archive)

90.   We are looking north from the level crossing to the junction on the same day. The line to St Ives diverges to the left, past the cottages and buildings dating back to the early days of the railway. There was once a station here, which was very short lived, opening and disappearing from the timetables in 1850. (NRS Archive)

91.   Now we have a driver's-eye view through the river bridge towards the signal box. This replaced the earlier signal box to the south of the level crossing, and survived until November 1984, some three months after this picture was taken. (D.C.Pearce)

92.　　After World War II the area seen in picture 87 was totally transformed by the construction of a modern permanent way depot. This 1967 view gives an idea of the scale of the operation, with the plant for producing long-welded rails to the left. (R.F.Bonny)

93.　　In addition to the miles of standard gauge track, a 2ft gauge system was used to transport lighter items around the yard. Here is one of the two Ruston & Hornsby diesel mechanical locomotives that operated on the narrow gauge lines. (R.Gooch)

94.   Considering the state of the art track equipment all around, the arrangements where the narrow and standard gauge lines crossed each other seemed rudimentary. However, the grooves cut into the standard gauge rails to accommodate narrow gauge wheel flanges were no doubt perfectly adequate for the task. (R.Gooch)

95.   An 0-6-0 diesel shunts wagons deep in the complex during 1967. This was one of two locos, Departmental nos 91 and 92, that worked here during the 1960s, replacing a pair of Sentinel steam shunters. By 2005 the depot had been abandoned for some years, and the whole area was engulfed in undergrowth, although a stone train occasionally used one of the sidings. (R.F.Bonny)

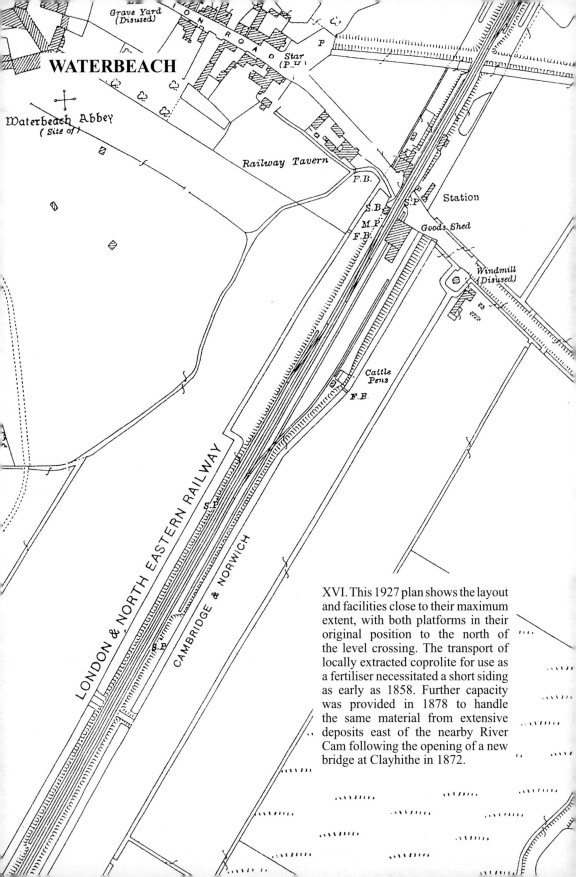

WATERBEACH

Grave Yard
(Disused)

Star
(P.H)

Waterbeach Abbey
(Site of)

Railway Tavern

F.B.

Station

S.B.

M.P.

F.B.

S.P.

Goods Shed

Windmill
(Disused)

Cattle
Pens

F.B.

LONDON & NORTH EASTERN RAILWAY

S.P.

CAMBRIDGE & NORWICH

S.B.

XVI. This 1927 plan shows the layout and facilities close to their maximum extent, with both platforms in their original position to the north of the level crossing. The transport of locally extracted coprolite for use as a fertiliser necessitated a short siding as early as 1858. Further capacity was provided in 1878 to handle the same material from extensive deposits east of the nearby River Cam following the opening of a new bridge at Clayhithe in 1872.

96.   As we look north from a signal post on 24th August 1911, a few passengers have congregated on the up platform.   However, the main activity is in the yard, where some twenty wagons are being handled in the goods shed and two sidings. The lime washed cattle pens are a reminder of another traffic flow, which could be heavy at certain times. (J. Watling collection)

97.   The station building stood on the down platform, and was similar to those at Shippea Hill and Lakenheath, to the east of Ely on the Eastern Counties Railway line to Brandon. This picture dates from the 1950s, when oil lamps still provided the platform lighting. (NRS Archive)

98.   Most passengers approach the station from the village to the west of the line. This is their view along the road towards the level crossing on 6th August 1967, with the station building to the left. (Railway Record of the British Isles/G.L.Pring)

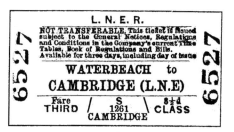

99.	On the same day, the combination of wooden goods shed, level crossing gates, crane and signal box produces a traditional scene. The yard had closed to goods traffic on 18th April 1966, a situation unimaginable when picture 96 was taken.
(Railway Record of the British Isles/G.L.Pring)

100.	A class 37 passes the station with train 1L23, an up express from Kings Lynn, on 4th August 1973. The blue enamel running-in boards and GER seats have been there for years, but the electric lighting is more recent. To the right of the engine, a gradient post indicates a summit, but in this part of the world, such things are comparatively insignificant. (R.Powell)

101.   As the twentieth century drew to a close, things changed considerably. On a wet day in 1996 we are looking north from a new up platform on the site of the goods shed, over the automated level crossing, to the down platform, where a "bus shelter" has replaced the station buildings. The little hut by the level crossing provides a link with picture 97. (A.C.Mott)

STRETHAM FEN

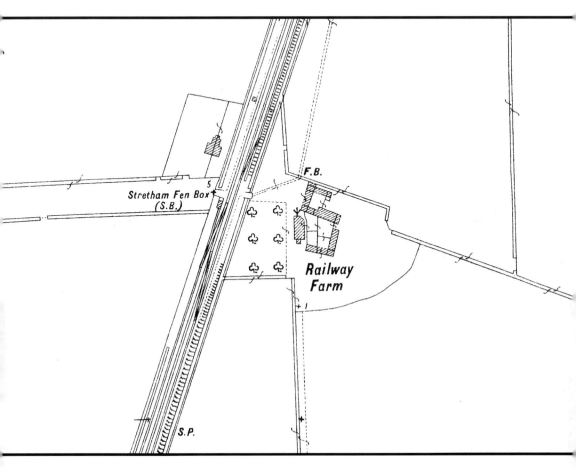

F.B.

Stretham Fen Box
(S.B.)

Railway
Farm

S.P.

XVII. This rather remote location was rarely, if ever, photographed. The signal box, about 4½ miles north of Waterbeach, was opened as a block post in 1876. A private siding was provided to cater for traffic from local farms in the mid-1920s as shown in this 1926 plan. The destruction of the signal box by fire in July 1966 brought about the closure of the up and down refuge sidings which were removed early in 1967.

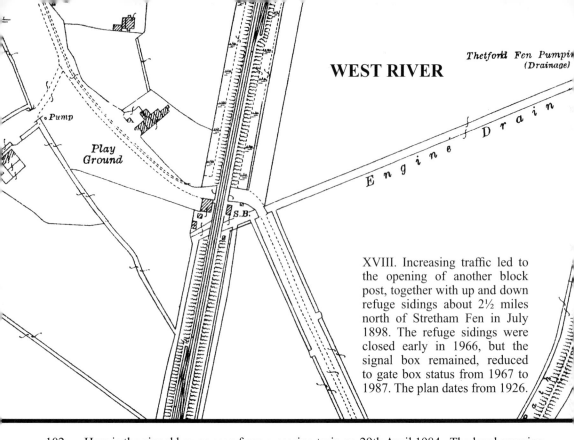

WEST RIVER

West River   *Thetford Fen Pumpi*
(Drainage)

Pump

Play Ground

S.B.

Engine Drain

XVIII. Increasing traffic led to the opening of another block post, together with up and down refuge sidings about 2½ miles north of Stretham Fen in July 1898. The refuge sidings were closed early in 1966, but the signal box remained, reduced to gate box status from 1967 to 1987. The plan dates from 1926.

102.   Here is the signal box as seen from a passing train on 29th April 1984. The level crossing gates protect a farm track, which crosses the railway and meanders across the countryside for a few hundred yards before petering out by the west bank of the River Great Ouse. (R.Powell)

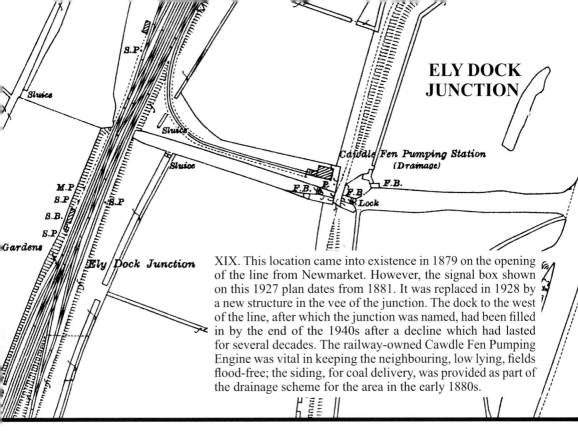

ELY DOCK JUNCTION

XIX. This location came into existence in 1879 on the opening of the line from Newmarket. However, the signal box shown on this 1927 plan dates from 1881. It was replaced in 1928 by a new structure in the vee of the junction. The dock to the west of the line, after which the junction was named, had been filled in by the end of the 1940s after a decline which had lasted for several decades. The railway-owned Cawdle Fen Pumping Engine was vital in keeping the neighbouring, low lying, fields flood-free; the siding, for coal delivery, was provided as part of the drainage scheme for the area in the early 1880s.

103.   As we approach our destination in April 1967, the line from Newmarket converges from the east to join the main line just north of the signal box. Some 25 years later the track layout was simplified and the traditional signalling abolished. (R.Powell)

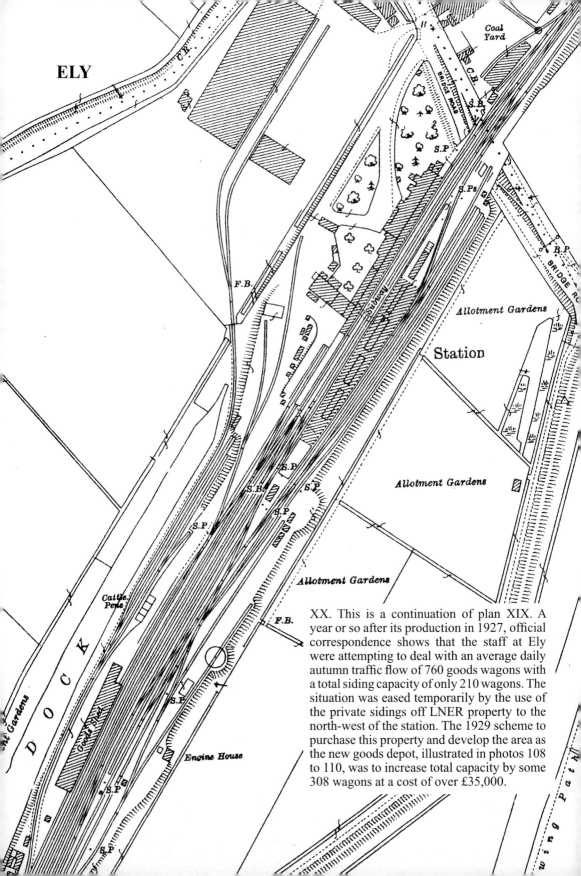

ELY

Coal Yard

Station

Allotment Gardens

Allotment Gardens

Allotment Gardens

Cattle Pens

D O C K

Goods Shed

Engine House

XX. This is a continuation of plan XIX. A year or so after its production in 1927, official correspondence shows that the staff at Ely were attempting to deal with an average daily autumn traffic flow of 760 goods wagons with a total siding capacity of only 210 wagons. The situation was eased temporarily by the use of the private sidings off LNER property to the north-west of the station. The 1929 scheme to purchase this property and develop the area as the new goods depot, illustrated in photos 108 to 110, was to increase total capacity by some 308 wagons at a cost of over £35,000.

104.   We go back to the early years of the twentieth century to find two horse-drawn carriages waiting outside the ornate frontage of the station. Members of the public and railway staff appear equally eager to be part of the picture. (Cambridgeshire Collection, Cambridge Central Library)

105.   Illuminated by low December sunshine, a GER 0-6-0T stands alongside the coal stage outside the locomotive shed in 1910, with a maze of trackwork leading to the station beyond. To the left of the signal box we can see the early goods shed, standing at right angles to the running line. Access to this was from a wagon turntable, an arrangement that became unworkable when the platform was extended southwards by some 300' in 1898. (J.Watling collection)

106.   This is the view southwards, probably looking from the signal box, on the same day. To our right a tank engine is shunting wagons in the goods shed, an imposing looking edifice, which had replaced the previous facility as a result of the 1898 changes. The engine shed, a long, corrugated iron structure, is on the left. (J.Watling collection)

107.   Here is the main station building in 1910, as seen from the island platform. The area shown was virtually the full extent of the platform until the 1898 extension was built. This lengthening brought about the demolition of an ornate footbridge, described in a contemporary plan as "The Gallery", which spanned the lines at the south end of the down platform.
(Lens of Sutton Collection)

108.   This view of the interior of the 1930s goods shed illustrates just how much general freight traffic the railway handled. A bewildering array of packages of all shapes and sizes are stacked up against the wall, and other items, including a consignment of wheelbarrows, occupy the platform.
(Cambridgeshire Collection, Cambridge Central Library)

109.   The exterior of the shed reveals an equally busy scene, with no fewer than six lorries, and a number of trailers, involved in transhipping goods between road and rail. All the lorries bear the LNER logo. (Cambridgeshire Collection, Cambridge Central Library)

G. E. R.
———
Ely

110.   Completing our look at the thriving goods depot - a rarely recorded aspect of the railway scene – we see an early "mechanical horse" demonstrating its ability to negotiate tight corners. No doubt it is involved in collection and delivery of packages around the city, and the variety and extent of its load deserves more than a passing glance.
(Cambridgeshire Collection, Cambridge Central Library)

111.   The signalman in the South box enjoyed a good view of the activity in both directions. We are looking northwards to the station, where one of the Kings Lynn "Claud Hamilton" 4-4-0s allocated to royal train duties has arrived at the outer face of the island platform. A train of Gresley coaches, complete with roof boards, occupies the down platform in this 1939 view, and the old goods shed is still standing to the left. (Stations UK)

112.   The engine shed had vanished by the 1920s, but the turntable and water tower continued to meet the needs of steam engines until the diesels took over entirely. Class D16/3 4-4-0 no.62566 is being turned, ready for its next duty, on 25th June 1958. (R.C.Riley / The Transport Treasury)

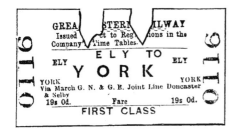

GREAT WESTERN RAILWAY
Issued subject to Regulations in the
Company's Time Tables.
    E L Y   T O
ELY Y O R K ELY
YORK   YORK
Via March G. N. & G. E. Joint Line Doncaster
& Selby
19s 0d.   Fare   19s 0d.
    FIRST CLASS

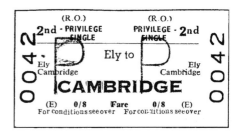

(R.O.)   (R.O.)
2nd - PRIVILEGE   PRIVILEGE - 2nd
    SINGLE   SINGLE
        Ely to
Ely   Ely
Cambridge   Cambridge
CAMBRIDGE
(E)   0/8   Fare   0/8   (E)
For conditions see over For conditions see over

113.   Another engine of the same class, no. 62615, passes the South signal box as it arrives with a train from the Cambridge direction in June 1958. (R.C.Riley / The Transport Treasury)

114.   With the cathedral in the background, class J17 0-6-0 no. 65578 waits with the Sutton goods train in the sidings to the south of the station. It is 28th July 1961, and we have already seen this train out on the branch in previous pictures. (R.Powell)

115.   Returning to the platform on the same day we find plenty of activity at the station. A Brush Type 2 diesel is ready to leave with an up passenger train, as a sister engine approaches with a northbound freight. A third member of the class waits in one of the loops with another goods train, while a 204 h.p. shunter busies itself in the sidings. To the left and right, LNER designed coaches contrast with the modern motive power. (R.Powell)

116.   By the early 1960s, the exterior of the station showed several modifications. A comparison with picture 104 shows that the removal of the pillars, arched windows and roof adornment has led to a far more functional appearance, even though the two-storey section to the left has scarcely changed. (H.Davies)

117.   A temporary shelter was provided to protect subway users from the elements while the island platform awning was being renewed in early 1964. We can see this short-lived feature behind the railwayman on 25th March. (J.Watling)

118.   We take our last look at the "old" Ely, as no. 37043 waits to depart with a Kings Lynn to Liverpool Street train on 29th March 1980. The familiar blue and white running in boards have made way for corporate "British Rail" replacements, but the semaphore signalling will survive for another twelve years, before Cambridge power box takes responsibility. (B.Harrison)

Other views of this station can be found in
Branch Lines around March
Ely to Kings Lynn and Ely to Norwich

119.   Class 5 4-6-0 no. 73096 waits to leave with a "Cathedrals Express" excursion, returning to Liverpool Street on 20th December 2003. This was one of a handful of steam-hauled specials to appear here in the forty-odd years since regular steam traction finished, and several enthusiasts have braved the bitter cold to record the occasion. (D.C.Pearce)

120.   As part of the 1992 rebuilding, the up platform was widened, and the former centre road became the down line. Here is the much-modified station on 16th August 2004, featuring trains from each of the three principal traffic flows. A class 158 on a cross-country working and EMU no. 365515 forming a Kings Lynn to Kings Cross train occupy the island platform faces, as no.170202 pauses on a Cambridge to Norwich service. (R.J.Adderson)

MP Middleton Press

EVOLVING THE ULTIMATE RAIL **ENCYCLOPEDIA**

Easebourne Lane, Midhurst, West Sussex.
GU29 9AZ   Tel:01730 813169

www.middletonpress.co.uk   email:info@middletonpress.co.uk

A-0 906520   B-1 873793   C-1 901706   D-1 904474

OOP Out of Print at time of printing - Please check current availability   **BROCHURE AVAILABLE SHOWING NEW TITLES**

A
Abergavenny to Merthyr C 91 5
Aldgate & Stepney Tramways B 70 7
Allhallows - Branch Line to A 62 2
Alton - Branch Lines to A 11 8
Andover to Southampton A 82 7
Ascot - Branch Lines around A 64 9
Ashburton - Branch Line to B 95 2
Ashford - Steam to Eurostar B 67 7
Ashford to Dover A 48 7
Austrian Narrow Gauge D 04 7
Avonmouth - BL around D 42 X
B
Banbury to Birmingham D 27 6
Barking to Southend C 80 X
Barnet & Finchley Tramways B 93 6
Barry - Branch Lines around D 50 0
Basingstoke to Salisbury A 89 4
Bath Green Park to Bristol C 36 2
Bath to Evercreech Junction A 60 6
Bath Tramways B 86 3
Battle over Portsmouth 1940 A 29 0
Battle over Sussex 1940 A 79 7
Bedford to Wellingborough D 31 4
Betwixt Petersfield & Midhurst A 94 0
Blitz over Sussex 1941-42 B 35 9
Bodmin - Branch Lines around B 83 9
Bognor at War 1939-45 B 59 6
Bombers over Sussex 1943-45 B 51 0
Bournemouth & Poole Trys B 47 2
Bournemouth to Evercreech Jn A 46 0
Bournemouth to Weymouth A 57 6
Bournemouth Trolleybuses C 10 9
Bradford Trolleybuses D 19 5
Brecon to Neath D 43 8
Brecon to Newport D 16 0
Brickmaking in Sussex B 19 7
Brightons Tramways B 02 2 OOP
Brighton to Eastbourne A 16 9
Brighton to Worthing A 03 7
Brighton Trolleybuses D 34 9
Bristols Tramways B 57 X
Bristol to Taunton D 03 9
Bromley South to Rochester B 23 5
Bude - Branch Line to B 29 4
Burnham to Evercreech Jn A 68 1
Burton & Ashby Tramways C 51 6
C
Camberwell & West Norwood Tys B 22 7
Cambridge to Ely D 55 1
Canterbury - Branch Lines around B 58 8
Cardiff Trolleybuses C 64 0
Caterham & Tattenham Corner B 25 1
Changing Midhurst C 15 X
Chard and Yeovil - BLs around C 30 3
Charing Cross to Dartford A 75 4
Charing Cross to Orpington A 96 7
Cheddar - Branch Line to B 90 1
Cheltenham to Andover C 43 5
Chesterfield Tramways D 37 3
Chesterfield Trolleybuses D 51 9
Chichester to Portsmouth A 14 2
Clapham & Streatham Trys B 97 9 OOP
Clapham Junction - 50 yrs C 06 0 OOP
Clapham Junction to Beckenham Jn B 36 7
Clevedon & Portishead - BLs to D 18 7
Collectors Trains, Trolleys & Trams D 29 2
Colonel Stephens D62 4
Cornwall Narrow Gauge D 56 X
Crawley to Littlehampton A 34 7
Cromer - Branch Lines around C 26 5
Croydons Tramways B 42 1
Croydons Trolleybuses B 73 1 OOP
Croydon to East Grinstead B 48 0
Crystal Palace (HL) & Catford Loop A 87 8
D
Darlington Trolleybuses D 33 0
Dartford to Sittingbourne B 34 0
Derby Tramways D 17 9
Derby Trolleybuses C 72 9
Derwent Valley - Branch Line to the D 06 3
Didcot to Banbury D 02 0
Didcot to Swindon C 84 2
Didcot to Winchester C 13 3
Douglas to Peel C 88 5
Douglas to Port Erin C 55 9
Douglas to Ramsey D 39 X
Dover's Tramways B 24 3
Dover to Ramsgate A 78 9

E
Ealing to Slough C 42 7
Eastbourne to Hastings A 27 4
East Cornwall Mineral Railways D 22 5
East Croydon to Three Bridges A 53 3
East Grinstead - Branch Lines to A 07 X
East Ham & West Ham Tramways B 52 9
East Kent Light Railway A 61 4
East London - Branch Lines of C 44 3
East London Line B 80 4
East Ridings Secret Resistance D 21 7
Edgware & Willesden Tramways C 18 4
Effingham Junction - BLs around A 74 6
Eltham & Woolwich Tramways B 74 X
Ely to Kings Lynn C 53 2
Ely to Norwich C 90 7
Embankment & Waterloo Tramways B 41 3
Enfield & Wood Green Trys C 03 6 OOP
Enfield Town & Palace Gates - BL to D 32 2
Epsom to Horsham A 30 4
Euston to Harrow & Wealdstone C 89 3
Exeter & Taunton Tramways B 32 4
Exeter to Barnstaple B 15 4
Exeter to Newton Abbot C 49 4
Exeter to Tavistock B 69 3
Exmouth - Branch Lines to B 00 6
F
Fairford - Branch Line to A 52 5
Falmouth, Helston & St. Ives - BL to C 74 5
Fareham to Salisbury A 67 3
Faversham to Dover B 05 7 OOP
Felixstowe & Aldeburgh - BL to D 20 9
Fenchurch Street to Barking C 20 6
Festiniog - 50 yrs of enterprise C 83 4
Festiniog in the Fifties B 68 5
Festiniog in the Sixties B 91 X
Finsbury Park to Alexandra Palace C 02 8
Frome to Bristol B 77 4
Fulwell - Trams, Trolleys & Buses D 11 X
G
Gloucester to Bristol D 35 7
Gloucester to Cardiff D 66 7
Gosport & Horndean Trys B 92 8
Gosport - Branch Lines around A 36 3
Great Yarmouth Tramways D 13 6
Greenwich & Dartford Tramways B 14 6 OOP
Guildford to Redhill A 63 0
H
Hammersmith & Hounslow Trys C 33 8
Hampshire Narrow Gauge D 36 5
Hampshire Waterways A 84 3 OOP
Hampstead & Highgate Tramways B 53 7
Harrow to Watford D 14 4
Hastings to Ashford A 37 1 OOP
Hastings Tramways B 18 9 OOP
Hastings Trolleybuses B 81 2 OOP
Hawkhurst - Branch Line to A 66 5
Hayling - Branch Line to A 12 6
Haywards Heath to Seaford A 28 2
Henley, Windsor & Marlow - BL to C77 X
Hereford to Newport C 54 3
Hitchin to Peterborough D 07 1
Holborn & Finsbury Tramways B 79 0
Holborn Viaduct to Lewisham A 81 9
Horsham - Branch Lines to A 02 9
Huddersfield Trolleybuses C 92 3
Hull Tramways D60 8
Hull Trolleybuses D 24 1
Huntingdon - Branch Lines around A 93 2
I
Ilford & Barking Tramways B 61 8
Ilford to Shenfield C 97 4
Ilfracombe - Branch Line to B 21 9
Ilkeston & Glossop Tramways D 40 3
Industrial Rlys of the South East A 09 6
Ipswich to Saxmundham C 41 9
Ipswich Trolleybuses D 59 4
Isle of Wight Lines - 50 yrs C 12 5
K
Kent & East Sussex Waterways A 72 X
Kent Narrow Gauge C 45 1
Kingsbridge - Branch Line to C 98 2
Kingston & Hounslow Loops A 83 5
Kingston & Wimbledon Tramways B 56 1
Kingswear - Branch Line to C 17 6
L
Lambourn - Branch Line to C 70 2
Launceston & Princetown - BL to C 19 2
Lewisham & Catford Tramways B 26 X OOP
Lewisham to Dartford A 92 4

Lines around Wimbledon B 75 8
Liverpool Street to Chingford D 01 2
Liverpool Street to Ilford C 34 6
Liverpool Tramways - Eastern C 04 4
Liverpool Tramways - Northern C 46 X
Liverpool Tramways - Southern C 23 0
London Bridge to Addiscombe B 20 0
London Bridge to East Croydon A 58 4
London Chatham & Dover Railway A 88 6
London Termini - Past and Proposed D 00 4
London to Portsmouth Waterways B 43 X
Longmoor - Branch Lines to A 41 X
Looe - Branch Line to C 22 2
Lyme Regis - Branch Line to A 45 2
Lynton - Branch Line to B 04 9
M
Maidstone & Chatham Tramways B 40 5
Maidstone Trolleybuses C 00 1 OOP
March - Branch Lines around B 09 X
Margate & Ramsgate Tramways C 52 4
Marylebone to Rickmansworth D49 7
Midhurst - Branch Lines around A 49 5
Midhurst - Branch Lines to A 01 0 OOP
Military Defence of West Sussex A 23 1
Military Signals, South Coast C 54 0
Minehead - Branch Line to A 80 0
Mitcham Junction Lines B 01 4
Mitchell & company C 59 1
Moreton-in-Marsh to Worcester D 26 8
Moretonhampstead - Branch Line to C 27 3
N
Newbury to Westbury C 66 4
Newport (IOW) - Branch Lines to A 26 6
Newquay - Branch Lines to C 71 0
Newton Abbot to Plymouth C 60 5
Northern France Narrow Gauge C 75 3
North East German Narrow Gauge D 44 6
North Kent Tramways B 44 8
North London Line B 94 4
North Woolwich - BLs around C 65 6
Norwich Tramways C 40 0
Nottinghamshire & Derbyshire T/B D 63 2
Nottinghamshire & Derbyshire T/W D 53 5
O
Orpington to Tonbridge B 03 0
Oxford to Bletchley D57 8
Oxford to Moreton-in-Marsh D 15 2
P
Paddington to Ealing C 37 0
Paddington to Princes Risborough C 81 8
Padstow - Branch Line to B 54 5
Plymouth - BLs around B 98 7
Plymouth to St. Austell C 63 X
Pontypool to Mountain Ash D 65 9
Porthmadog 1954-94 - BL around B 31 6
Porthmadog to Blaenau B 50 2 OOP
Portmadoc 1923-46 - BL around B 13 8
Portsmouths Tramways B 72 3 OOP
Portsmouth to Southampton A 31 2
Portsmouth Trolleybuses C 73 7
Princes Risborough - Branch Lines to D 05 5
Princes Risborough to Banbury C 85 0
R
Railways to Victory C 16 8/7 OOP
Reading to Basingstoke B 27 8
Reading to Didcot C 79 6
Reading to Guildford A 47 9 OOP
Reading Tramways B 87 1
Reading Trolleybuses C 05 2
Redhill to Ashford A 73 8
Return to Blaenau 1970-82 C 64 8
Rickmansworth to Aylesbury D 61 6
Roman Roads of Hampshire D 67 5
Roman Roads of Surrey C 61 3
Roman Roads of Sussex C 48 6
Romneyrail C 32 X
Ryde to Ventnor A 19 3
S
Salisbury to Westbury B 39 1
Salisbury to Yeovil B 06 5
Saxmundham to Yarmouth C 69 9
Saxony Narrow Gauge D 47 0
Seaton & Eastbourne Tramways B 76 6
Seaton & Sidmouth - Branch Lines to A 95 9
Secret Sussex Resistance B 82 0
SECR Centenary album C 11 7
Selsey - Branch Line to A 04 5
Sheerness - Branch Lines around B 16 2
Shepherds Bush to Uxbridge T/Ws C 28 1
Shrewsbury - Branch Lines to A 86 X

Sierra Leone Narrow Gauge D 28 4
Sittingbourne to Ramsgate A 90 8
Slough to Newbury C 56 7
Solent - Creeks, Crafts & Cargoes D 52
Southamptons Tramways B 33 2 OOP
Southampton to Bournemouth A 42 8
Southend-on-Sea Tramways B 28 6
Southern France Narrow Gauge C 47
Southwark & Deptford Tramways B 3
Southwold - Branch Line to A 15 0
South Eastern & Chatham Railways C
South London Line B 46 4
South London Tramways 1903-33 D 10
St. Albans to Bedford D 08 X
St. Austell to Penzance C 67 2
St. Pancras to Barking D 68 3
St. Pancras to St. Albans C 78 8
Stamford Hill Tramways B 85 5
Steaming through Cornwall B 30 8
Steaming through Kent A 13 4 OOP
Steaming through the Isle of Wight A 5
Steaming through West Hants A 69 X
Stratford-upon-Avon to Cheltenham C
Strood to Paddock Wood B 12 X
Surrey Home Guard C 57 5
Surrey Narrow Gauge C 87 7
Surrey Waterways A 51 7 OOP
Sussex Home Guard C 24 9
Sussex Narrow Gauge C 50 8
Sussex Shipping Sail, Steam & Motor
Swanley to Ashford B 45 6
Swindon to Bristol C 96 6
Swindon to Gloucester D46 2
Swindon to Newport D 30 6
Swiss Narrow Gauge C 94 X
T
Talyllyn - 50 years C 39 7
Taunton to Barnstaple B 60 X
Taunton to Exeter C 82 6
Tavistock to Plymouth B 88 X
Tees-side Trolleybuses D 58 6
Tenterden - Branch Line to A 21 5
Thanet's Tramways B 11 1 OOP
Three Bridges to Brighton A 35 5
Tilbury Loop C 86 9
Tiverton - Branch Lines around C 62 1
Tivetshall to Beccles D 41 1
Tonbridge to Hastings A 44 4
Torrington - Branch Lines to B 37 5
Tunbridge Wells - Branch Lines to A 32 7
Twickenham & Kingston Trys C 35 4
Two-Foot Gauge Survivors C 21 4 OO
U
Upwell - Branch Line to B 64 2
V
Victoria & Lambeth Tramways B 49 9
Victoria to Bromley South A 98 3
Victoria to East Croydon A 40 1
Vivarais C 31 1
W
Walthamstow & Leyton Tramways B 6
Waltham Cross & Edmonton Trys C 0
Wandsworth & Battersea Tramways B
Wantage - Branch Line to D 25 X
Wareham to Swanage - 50 yrs D 09 8
War on the Line A 10 X
War on the Line VIDEO + 88 0
Waterloo to Windsor A 54 1
Waterloo to Woking A 38 X
Watford to Leighton Buzzard D 45 4
Wenford Bridge to Fowey C 09 5
Westbury to Bath B 55 3
Westbury to Taunton C 76 1
West Cornwall Mineral Railways D 48
West Croydon to Epsom B 08 1
West London - Branch Lines of C 50 8
West London Line B 84 7
West Sussex Waterways A 24 X
West Wiltshire - Branch Lines of D 12 8
Weymouth - Branch Lines around A 65
Willesden Junction to Richmond B 71 5
Wimbledon to Beckenham C 58 3
Wimbledon to Epsom B 62 6
Wimborne - Branch Lines around A 97
Wisbech - Branch Lines around C 01 X
Wisbech 1800-1901 C 93 1
Woking to Alton A 59 2
Woking to Portsmouth A 25 8
Woking to Southampton A 55 X
Woolwich & Dartford Trolleys B 66 9
Worcester to Hereford D 38 1
Worthing to Chichester A 06 1
Y
Yeovil - 50 yrs change C 38 9
Yeovil to Dorchester A 76 2 OOP
Yeovil to Exeter A 91 6